A TREASURY of POEMS for CHILDREN

A TREASURY of POEMS for CHILDREN

Selected by **M. G. EDGAR**

ILLUSTRATED BY
WILLY·POGÁNY

Dover Publications, Inc., Mineola, New York

Bibliographical Note

This Dover edition, first published in 2009, is a republication of the work originally published by George G. Harrap & Co., London, ca. 1912. The original color plates have been gathered together as an eight-page color insert between pp. 30 and 31.

Library of Congress Cataloging-in-Publication Data

Treasury of verse for little children
    A treasury of poems for children / selected by M.G. Edgar ; illustrated by Willy Pogány.
       p. cm.
    "Republication of the work originally published by George G. Harrap & Co., London, ca. 1912"—T.p. verso.
    ISBN-13: 978-0-486-47376-5
    ISBN-10: 0-486-47376-7
    1. Children's poetry, English. 2. Children's poetry, American. I. Edgar, M. G. (Madalen G.) II. Pogány, Willy, 1882-1955, ill. III. Title.

PR1175.3.T74 2009
821.008'09282—dc22

2009022799

Manufactured in the United States by Courier Corporation
47376701
www.doverpublications.com

PREFATORY NOTE

THE COMPILER desires to offer thanks to authors and owners of copyright poems for permission to use the following in this Collection. To:

Mrs. Allingham for *The Fairies, Robin Redbreast,* and *Wishing,* by Wm. Allingham; Miss M. Betham-Edwards for *A Child's Hymn;* Messrs. Bickers and Son for *The Elf and the Dormouse,* by Oliver Herford; The Bobbs-Merrill Company for *A Sea-Song from the Shore,* by James Whitcomb Riley; Mrs. Hubert Brand for *Baby Seed Song;* Miss Kate Louise Brown for *Dandelion* and *The Tree Buds;* Mr. William Canton for *She was a Treasure, she was a Sweet;* Messrs. Chatto and Windus for *Baby* and *The Wind and the Moon,* by Dr. George MacDonald; Mrs. Eden and Mrs. Ward for *A Friend in the Garden, Big Smith,* and *The Willow-Man,* by Mrs. J. H. Ewing; Mr. Norman Gale for *The Fairy Book* and *Mustard and Cress;* Messrs. Houghton, Mifflin & Co. for *Discontent,* by Sarah Orne Jewett; *The Brown Thrush,* by Lucy Larcom; *Daisies,* by Frank Dempster Sherman; *A Night with a Wolf,* by Bayard Taylor; *Chanticleer,* by Celia Thaxter; and

5

The CHILDREN'S TREASURY

The Sandman, by Margaret Vandegrift; Mr. John Lane and Messrs. Charles Scribner's Sons for *Wynken, Blynken, and Nod*, by Eugene Field; Mr. John Lane for *Wonderful World*, by Wm. B. Rands; and *The World's Music*, by Gabriel Setoun; Messrs. Longmans, Green & Co. for *Foreign Lands, The Lamplighter*, and *The Little Land*, from "A Child's Garden of Verse," by Robert Louis Stevenson; Mr. E. V. Lucas for *Snow in Town*, by Rickman Mark; Messrs. Macmillan & Co., Ltd., for *The Walrus and the Carpenter*, from "Through the Looking-Glass," by Lewis Carroll; Judge Parry for *I would like you for a Comrade;* Laura E. Richards for *Prince Tatters* and *A Nursery Song;* Mrs. Annie D. G. Robinson for *A Good Thanksgiving* and *Little Sorrow*, by Marion Douglas; Messrs. Charles Scribner's Sons for *One, Two, Three*, by Henry Cuyler Bunner; Messrs. F. Warne and Co. for *The Owl and the Pussy Cat*, from "Nonsense Songs and Stories," by Edward Lear; Miss Anna B. Warner for *Daffy-Down-Dilly;* and Mr. Fred. E. Weatherly for *The Gray Doves' Answer*.

CONTENTS

The CHILDREN'S TREASURY

The CHILDREN'S TREASURY

The CHILDREN'S TREASURY

Foreign Lands

Up into the cherry tree
Who should climb but little me?
I held the trunk with both my hands
And looked abroad on foreign lands.

I saw the next door garden lie,
Adorned with flowers, before my eye,
And many pleasant places more
That I had never seen before.

I saw the dimpling river pass
And be the sun's blue looking-glass ;
The dusty roads go up and down
With people tramping in to town.

If I could find a higher tree
Farther and farther I should see,
To where the grown-up river slips
Into the sun among the ships,

To where the roads on either hand
Lead onward into fairy land,
Where all the children dine at five,
And all the playthings come alive.

Robert Louis Stevenson

The Tree Buds

ROCK-A-BY, Baby,
Up in a tree,
Rock-a-by, baby,
What can we see?

Little brown cradles?
Yes, that is all;
Little brown cradles
Never will fall.

Where are the babies?
Oh! they are there,
Tucked in their blankets
Away from the air.

Dear little nurslings,
Quiet all day,
In their green nightgowns
Folded away.

North wind is piping
Loud lullaby;
He couldn't soften
His voice, did he try.

Sleep till the springtime
Brightens the sky.
Little leaf babies,
We love you.　Good-bye.

Kate Louise Brown

Long Time ago

ONCE there was a little kitty,
   White as the snow ;
In a barn she used to frolic
   Long time ago.

In the barn a little mousie
   Ran to and fro,
For she heard the little kitty
   Long time ago.

Two black eyes had little kitty,
   Black as a sloe ;
And they spied the little mousie
   Long time ago.

Four soft paws had little kitty,
   Paws soft as snow ;
And they caught the little mousie
   Long time ago.

Nine pearl teeth had little kitty,
   All in a row ;
And they bit the little mousie
   Long time ago.

When the teeth bit little mousie,
   Mousie cried out, "Oh !"
But she slipped away from kitty
   Long time ago.

Unknown

She was a Treasure

HE was a treasure ; she was a
    sweet ;
She was the darling of the Army
    and the Fleet !

When—she—smiled
The crews of the line-of-battle ships went
    wild !

When—she—cried—
Whole regiments reversed their arms and
  sighed !

When she was sick, for her sake
The Queen took off her crown and sobbed as
  if her heart would break.

William Canton

· Daisies ·

T evening when I go to bed
I see the stars shine overhead ;
They are the little daisies white
That dot the meadow of the
night.

And often while I m dreaming so,
Across the sky the moon will go ;
It is a lady, sweet and fair,
Who comes to gather daisies there.

For, when at morning I arise,
There's not a star left in the skies ;
  She's picked them all and dropped them
    down
  Into the meadows of the town.

Frank Dempster Sherman

*By special arrangement with Messrs. Houghton,
Mifflin & Co., the authorised publishers of
Mr. Sherman's Poems*

The Rainbow Fairies

TWO little clouds one summer's
    day
    Went flying through the sky.
    They went so fast they bumped
  their heads,
And both began to cry.

Old Father Sun looked out and said,
  " Oh, never mind, my dears,
I'll send my little fairy folk
  To dry your falling tears."

One fairy came in violet,
    And one in indigo,
In blue, green, yellow, orange, red,—
    They made a pretty row.

They wiped the cloud tears all away,
    And then, from out the sky,
Upon a line the sunbeams made,
    They hung their gowns to dry.

Lizzie M. Hadley

The New Moon

 DEAR mother, how pretty
    The moon looks to-night !
    She was never so lovely before ;
    Her two little horns
  Are so sharp and so bright,
I hope she'll not grow any more.

  If I were up there
  With you and my friends,
I'd rock in it nicely you'd see,

I'd sit in the middle
And hold by both ends ;
Oh, what a bright cradle 'twould be!

I would call to the stars
To keep out of the way,
Lest we should rock over their toes ;
And there I would rock
Till the dawn of the day,
And see where the pretty moon goes.

And there we would stay
In the beautiful skies,
And through the bright clouds we would
roam ;
We would see the sun set,
And see the sun rise,
And on the next rainbow come home.

Eliza L. C. Follen

The Elf and the Dormouse

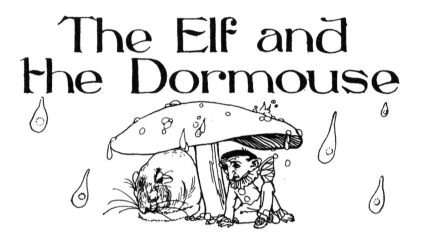

 NDER a toadstool
    Crept a wee Elf,
Out of the rain
    To shelter himself.

Under the toadstool,
    Sound asleep,
Sat a big Dormouse
    All in a heap.

'Good Gracious Me! Where Is My Toadstool?'

Trembled the wee Elf,
   Frightened, and yet
Fearing to fly away
   Lest he got wet.

To the next shelter—
   Maybe a mile!
Sudden the wee Elf
   Smiled a wee smile.

Tugged till the toadstool
   Toppled in two.
Holding it over him,
   Gaily he flew.

Soon he was safe home,
   Dry as could be.
Soon woke the Dormouse—
   " Good gracious me!

"Where is my toadstool?"
   Loud he lamented.
And that's how umbrellas
   First were invented.

Oliver Herford

COLOR PLATES

Good Night and Good Morning
[page 31]

The Fairy Folk
[page 119]

The Owl and the Pussy-Cat
[page 156]

Big Smith
[page 159]

The Fairies
[page 163]

The Walrus and the Carpenter
[page 228]

The Fairies of the Caldon Low
[page 235]

GOODNIGHT and GOODMORNING

A fair little girl sat under a tree,
Sewing as long as her eyes could see:

Then smoothed her work, and folded it right,
And said, " Dear work, Good-Night! Good-
Night! "

Such a number of rooks came over her head,
Crying, "Caw! caw!" on their way to bed :
She said, as she watched their curious flight,
" Little black things, Good-Night! Good-
Night!"

The horses neighed, and the oxen lowed,
The sheep's " Bleat! bleat!" came over the
road :
All seeming to say, with a quiet delight,
" Good little girl, Good-night! Good-night!"

She did not say to the sun, "Good-night!"
Though she saw him there like a ball of
light ;
For she knew he had God's time to keep
All over the world, and never could sleep.

The tall pink foxglove bowed his head—
The violet curtsied and went to bed ;
And good little Lucy tied up her hair,
And said on her knees her favourite prayer.

And while on her pillow she softly lay,
She knew nothing more till again it was day :
And all things said to the beautiful sun,
" Good-Morning ! Good-Morning ! our work
  is begun ! "

Lord Houghton

"Good-Morning ! Good-morning ! our work is begun !"

The Lost Doll

 ONCE had a sweet little doll,
        dears,
    The prettiest doll in the world ;
Her cheeks were so red and so
        white, dears,
And her hair was so charmingly curled.
But I lost my poor little doll, dears,
    As I played in the heath one day ;
And I cried for her more than a week, dears ;
    But I never could find where she lay.

The CHILDREN'S TREASURY

I found my poor little doll, dears,
  As I played in the heath one day;
Folks say she is terribly changed, dears,
  For her paint is all washed away,
And her arms trodden off by the cows, dears,
  And her hair not the least bit curled:
Yet for old sakes' sake she is still, dears,
  The prettiest doll in the world.

Charles Kingsley

one, two, three

T was an old, old, old, old lady,
   And a boy that was half-past
      three,
   And the way that they played
  together
Was beautiful to see.

She couldn't go romping and jumping,
   And the boy no more could he,
For he was a thin little fellow,
   With a thin little twisted knee.

They sat in the yellow sunlight,
  Out under the maple tree,
And the game that they played I'll tell you,
  Just as it was told to me.

It was Hide-and-Go-Seek they were playing
  Though you'd never have known it to be—
With an old, old, old, old lady,
  And a boy with a twisted knee.

The boy would bend his face down
  On his little sound right knee,
And he guessed where she was hiding
  In guesses, One, Two, Three.

" You are in the china closet ! "
  He would laugh and cry with glee—
It wasn't the china closet,
  But he still had Two and Three.

" You are up in papa's big bedroom,
  In the chest with the queer old key,"
And she said : " You are warm and warmer ;
  But you are not quite right," said she.

" It can't be the little cupboard
　Where mamma's things used to be—
So it must be in the clothes-press, gran'ma,"
　And he found her with his Three.

Then she covered her face with her fingers,
　That were wrinkled and white and wee,
And she guessed where the boy was hiding,
　With a One and a Two and a Three.

And they never had stirred from their places
　Right under the maple tree—
This old, old, old, old lady
　And the boy with the lame little knee—
This dear, dear, dear, dear old lady,
　And the boy who was half-past three.

Henry Cuyler Bunner

*From " Poems of H. C. Bunner " ; copyright
1884, 1892, 1899, by Charles Scribner's Sons.*

A Boy's Song

WHERE the pools are bright and
    deep,
Where the gray trout lies asleep,
Up the river and o'er the lea—
That's the way for Billy and me.

Where the blackbird sings the latest,
Where the hawthorn blooms the sweetest,
Where the nestlings chirp and flee—
That's the way for Billy and me.

Where the mowers mow the cleanest,
Where the hay lies thick and greenest ;
There to trace the homeward bee—
That's the way for Billy and me.

Where the hazel bank is steepest,
Where the shadow lies the deepest,
Where the clustering nuts fall free—
That's the way for Billy and me.

Why the boys should drive away
Little sweet maidens from the play,
Or love to banter and fight so well,
That's the thing I never could tell.

But this I know : I love to play,
Through the meadow, among the hay
Up the water and o'er the lea,
That's the way for Billy and me.

James Hogg

Dandelion

I SAW him peeping from my lawn,
  A tiny spot of yellow,
His face was one substantial
      smile—
The jolly little fellow.

I think he wore a doublet green,
  His golden skirt tucked under;
He carried, too, a sword so sharp
  That I could only wonder.

"Are you a soldier, little man,
  You, with your face so sunny?"
The fellow answered not a word;
  I thought it very funny.

I left him there to guard my lawn
　　From robins bent on plunder,
The soldier lad with doublet green,
　　His yellow skirt tucked under.

The days passed on—one afternoon
　　As I was out a-walking,
Whom should I meet upon the lawn
　　But soldier lad a-stalking.

His head, alas! was white as snow,
　　And it was all a-tremble;
Ah! scarce did this old veteran
　　My bonny lad resemble.

I bent to speak with pitying word—
　　Alas! for good intention;
His snowy locks blew quite away—
　　The rest we will not mention.

　　　　　　Kate Louise Brown

The Butterfly's Ball

OME, take up your hats, and
    away let us haste
    To the Butterfly's Ball and the
    Grasshopper's Feast ;
The trumpeter, Gadfly, has summoned the
    crew,
And the revels are now only waiting for you."

So said little Robert, and pacing along,
His merry companions came forth in a throng,
And on the smooth grass by the side of a
    wood,
Beneath a broad oak that for ages has stood,
Saw the children of earth and the tenants of
    air
For an evening's amusement together repair.

45

And there came the Beetle, so blind and so
   black,
Who carried the Emmet, his friend, on his
   back ;
And there was the Gnat and the Dragon-fly
   too,
With all their relations, green, orange, and
   blue.

And there came the Moth, with his plumage
   of down,
And the Hornet, in jacket of yellow and
   brown,
Who with him the Wasp, his companion, did
   bring :
They promised that evening to lay by their
   sting.

And the sly little Dormouse crept out oᶠ his
   hole,
And brought to the Feast his blind brother,
   the Mole.
And the Snail, with his horns peeping out of
   his shell,
Came from a great distance—the length of an
   ell.

A mushroom their table, and on it was laid
A water-dock leaf, which a table-cloth made.
The viands were various, to each of their
    taste,
And the Bee brought her honey to crown the
    repast.

Then close on his haunches, so solemn and
    wise,
The Frog from a corner looked up to the
    skies;
And the Squirrel, well-pleased such diversions
    to see,
Mounted high overhead and looked down from
    a tree.

Then out came a Spider, with fingers so fine,
To show his dexterity on the tight-line.
From one branch to another his cobwebs he
    slung,
Then quick as an arrow he darted along.

But just in the middle—oh! shocking to
    tell,
From his rope, in an instant, poor Harlequin
    fell.

Yet he touched not the ground, but with
talons outspread,
Hung suspended in air, at the end of a
thread.

Then the Grasshopper came, with a jerk and
a spring,
Very long was his leg, though but short was
his wing ;
He took but three leaps, and was soon out of
sight,
Then chirped his own praises the rest of the
night.

With step so majestic, the Snail did advance,
And promised the gazers a minuet to
dance :
But they all laughed so loud that he pulled in
his head,
And went to his own little chamber to bed.
Then as evening gave way to the shadows of
night,
Their watchman, the Glow-worm, came out
with a light.

With step so majestic, the Snail did advance,
And promised the gazers a minuet to dance:

The CHILDREN'S TREASURY

"Then home let us hasten while yet we can
    see,
For no watchman is waiting for you and for
    me."
So said little Robert, and pacing along,
His merry companions returned in a throng.

William Roscoe

Wishing

ING-TING! I wish I were a
      primrose,
   A bright yellow primrose blowing
      in the spring!
    The stooping boughs above me,
  The wandering bee to love me,
The fern and moss to creep across,
   And the elm-tree for our king!

Nay, stay! I wish I were an elm-tree,
A great lofty elm-tree, with green leaves gay!
    The winds would set them dancing,
    The sun and moonshine glance in,
And birds would house among the boughs,
    And sweetly sing!

Oh—no! I wish I were a robin,
A robin or a little wren, everywhere to go ;
    Through forest, field or garden,
    And ask no leave or pardon,
Till winter comes with icy thumbs
    To ruffle up our wing.

Well—tell! Where should I fly to,
Where go to sleep in the dark wood or dell?
    Before a day was over,
    Home comes the rover,
For mother's kiss—sweeter this,
    Than any other thing!

William Allingham

Putting the World to Bed

THE little snow people are hurrying down
 From their home in the clouds overhead ;
They are working as hard as ever they can,
 Putting the world to bed.

Every tree in a soft fleecy nightgown they clothe ;
 Each part has its night-cap of white.
And o'er the cold ground a thick cover they spread
 Before they say good-night.

And so they come eagerly sliding down,
 With a swift and silent tread,
Always as busy as busy can be,
 Putting the world to bed.

Esther W. Buxton

53

Santa Claus

 E comes in the night! He comes in
  the night!
 He softly, silently comes;
While the little brown heads on
 the pillows so white
Are dreaming of bugles and drums.

He cuts through the snow like a ship through
 the foam,
 While the white flakes around him whirl;
Who tells him I know not, but he findeth the
 home
 Of each good little boy and girl.

54

His sleigh it is long, and deep, and wide ;
　It will carry a host of things,
While dozens of drums hang over the side,
　With the sticks sticking under the strings.
And yet not the sound of a drum is heard,
　Not a bugle blast is blown,
As he mounts to the chimney-top like a
　bird,
　And drops to the hearth like a stone.

The little red stockings he silently fills,
　Till the stockings will hold no more ;
The bright little sleds for the great snow
　hills
　Are quickly set down on the floor.
Then Santa Claus mounts to the roof like a
　bird,
　And glides to his seat in the sleigh ;
Not the sound of a bugle or drum is heard
　As he noiselessly gallops away.

He rides to the East, and he rides to the
　West,
　Of his goodies he touches not one ;
He eateth the crumbs of the Christmas feast
　When the dear little folks are done.

The CHILDREN'S TREASURY

Old Santa Claus doeth all that he can ;
  This beautiful mission is his ;
Then, children, be good to the little old man,
  When you find who the little man is.

Unknown

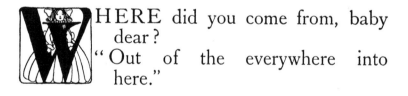

WHERE did you come from, baby dear?
"Out of the everywhere into here."

Where did you get those eyes so blue?
"Out of the sky as I came through."

What makes the light in them sparkle and
    spin ?
" Some of the starry spikes left in."

Where did you get that little tear ?
" I found it waiting when I got here."

What makes your forehead so smooth and
    high ?
" A soft hand stroked it as I went by."

What makes your cheek like a warm white
    rose ?
" I saw something better than any one knows ? "

Whence that three-cornered smile of bliss ?
" Three angels gave me at once a kiss."

Where did you get this pearly ear ?
"God spoke, and it came out to hear."

Where did you get those arms and hands ?
" Love made itself into bonds and bands."

Feet, whence did you come, you darling
    things ?
" From the same box as the cherubs' wings."

How did they all just come to be you ?
" God thought about me, and so I grew."

But how did you come to us, you dear ?
" God thought about you, and so I am here."

                   George MacDonald

Twinkle, Twinkle, Little Star,

TWINKLE, twinkle, little star,
How I wonder what you are!
Up above the world so high
Like a diamond in the sky.

When the blazing sun is gone,
When he nothing shines upon,
Then you show your little light,
Twinkle, twinkle, all the night.

61

Then the traveller in the dark
Thanks you for your tiny spark !
He could not see which way to go,
If you did not twinkle so.

In the dark blue sky you keep,
And often through my curtains peep,
For you never shut your eye
Till the sun is in the sky.

As your bright and tiny spark
Lights the traveller in the dark,
Though I know not what you are,
Twinkle, twinkle, little star.

Jane Taylor

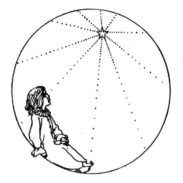

Then the traveller in the dark,
Thanks you for your tiny spark!

REAT, wide, beautiful, wonderful
World,
With the wonderful water round
you curled,
And the wonderful grass upon your breast—
World, you are beautifully drest.

The wonderful air is over me,
And the wonderful wind is shaking the tree,

It walks on the water, and whirls the mills,
And talks to itself on the tops of the hills.

You friendly Earth ! how far do you go,
With the wheat-fields that nod and the rivers
    that flow,
With cities, and gardens, and cliffs, and isles,
And people upon you for thousands of miles ?

Ah, you are so great, and I am so small,
I tremble to think of you, World, at all ;
And yet, when I said my prayers to-day,
A whisper inside me seemed to say,
"You are more than the Earth, though you
    are such a dot :
You can love and think, and the Earth cannot!"
                William Brighty Rands

Buttercups and Daisies

UTTERCUPS and Daisies—
　　Oh, the pretty flowers,
　　Coming ere the spring time
　　　To tell of sunny hours.
While the trees are leafless,
　While the fields are bare,
Buttercups and Daisies
　Spring up here and there.

Little hardy flowers
　Like to children poor,
Playing in their sturdy health
　By their mother's door;

Purple with the north wind,
  Yet alert and bold,
Fearing not and caring not,
  Though they may be cold.

What to them is weather?
  What are stormy showers?
Buttercups and Daisies
  Are these human flowers.
He who gave them hardship
  And a life of care,
Gave them likewise hardy strength
  And patient hearts to bear.

Mary Howitt

A Nursery Song

OH, Peterkin Pout and Gregory Grout
    Are two little goblins black.
Full oft from my house I've driven
        them out,
But somehow they still come back.

They clamber up to the baby's mouth,
    And pull the corners down ;
They perch aloft on the baby's brow,
    And twist it into a frown.

And one says "Must!" and t'other says
*   "Can't!"*
And one says "Shall!" and t'other says
*   "Sha'n't!"*
Oh, Peterkin Pout and Gregory Grout,
I pray you now, from my house keep out!

But Samuel Smile and Lemuel Laugh
    Are two little fairies light;
They're always ready for fun and chaff,
    And sunshine is their delight.

And when they creep into Baby's eyes,
    Why, there the sunbeams are;
And when they peep through her rosy lips,
    Her laughter rings near and far.

And one says "Please!" and t'other says
*   "Do!"*
And both together say "I love you!"
So, Lemuel Laugh and Samuel Smile,
Come in, my dears, and tarry awhile!
*   Laura E. Richards*

The WORLD'S MUSIC

THE world's a very happy place,
   Where every child should laugh
      and sing,
And always have a smiling face,
   And never sulk for anything.

I waken when the morning's come,
   And feel the air and light alive
With strange sweet music, like the hum
   Of bees about their busy hive.

The linnets play among the leaves
   At hide-and-seek, and chirp and sing;
While, flashing to and from the eaves,
   The swallows twitter on the wing.

And twigs that shake, and boughs that sway,
   And tall old trees you could not climb,
And winds that come, but cannot stay,
   Are singing gaily all the time.

From dawn to dark the old mill-wheel
   Makes music, going round and round;
And dusty-white with flour and meal,
   The miller whistles to its sound.

The brook that flows beside the mill,
   As happy as a brook can be,
Goes singing its own song until
   It learns the singing of the sea.

For every wave upon the sands
   Sings songs you never tire to hear,
Of laden ships from sunny lands,
   Where it is summer all the year.

And if you listen to the rain
    When leaves and birds and bees are dumb,
You hear it pattering on the pane,
    Like Andrew beating on his drum.

The coals beneath the kettle croon,
    And clap their hands and dance in glee ;
And even the kettle hums a tune
    To tell you when it's time for tea.

The world is such a happy place
    That children, whether big or small,
Should always have a smiling face,
    And never, never sulk at all.

                              Gabriel Setoun

How doth the little busy Bee

OW doth the little busy bee
Improve each shining hour,
And gather honey all the day
From every opening flower!

How skilfully she builds her cell!
How neat she spreads the wax!
And labours hard to store it well
With the sweet food she makes.

In works of labour or of skill,
I would be busy too;
For Satan finds some mischief still
For idle hands to do.

In books, or work, or healthful play,
Let my first years be past,
That I may give for every day
Some good account at last.

Isaac Watts

A Child's hymn

OD make my life a little light,
   Within the world to glow;
A little flame that burneth bright,
   Wherever I may go.

God make my life a little flower,
   That giveth joy to all,
Content to bloom in native bower,
   Although the place be small.

God make my life a little song,
  That comforteth the sad ;
That helpeth others to be strong,
  And makes the singer glad.

God make my life a little staff,
  Whereon the weak may rest,
That so what health and strength
    I have
  May serve my neighbours best.

God make my life a little hymn
  Of tenderness and praise ;
Of faith, that never waxeth dim,
  In all His wondrous ways.

M. Betham-Edwards

Daffy-Down-Dilly

AFFY-DOWN-DILLY
Came up in the cold,
Through the brown mould,
Although the March breezes
Blew keen on her face,
Although the white snow
Lay on many a place.

Daffy-down-dilly
Had heard under ground,
The sweet rushing sound
Of the streams, as they broke
From their white winter chains,
Of the whistling spring winds
And the pattering rains.

"Now then," thought Daffy,
    Deep down in her heart,
    "It's time I should start."
So she pushed her soft leaves
    Through the hard frozen ground,
Quite up to the surface,
    And then she looked round.

There was snow all about her,
    Grey clouds over-head ;
    The trees all looked dead :
Then how do you think
    Poor Daffy-down felt,
When the sun would not shine,
    And the ice would not melt ?

"Cold weather!" thought Daffy,
    Still working away ;
    "The earth's hard to-day !
There's but a half inch
    Of my leaves to be seen,
And two-thirds of that
    Is more yellow than green.

" I can't do much yet,
But I'll do what I can :
It's well I began !
For unless I can manage
To lift up my head,
The people will think
That the Spring herself's dead."

So, little by little,
She brought her leaves out,
All clustered about ;
And then her bright flowers
Began to unfold,
Till Daffy stood robed
In her spring green and gold.

O Daffy-down-dilly,
So brave and so true !
I wish all were like you !—
So ready for duty
In all sorts of weather,
And loyal to courage
And duty together.

Anna B. Warner

The Fairy Book

 N Summer, when the grass is thick,
     if mother has the time,
She shows me with her pencil how
     a poet makes a rhyme,
And often she is sweet enough to
     choose a leafy nook,
Where I cuddle up so closely when she reads
     the Fairy-book.

In winter when the corn's asleep, and birds
     are not in song,
And crocuses and violets have been away too
     long,

Dear mother puts her thimble by in answer to
my look,
And I cuddle up so closely when she reads
the Fairy-book.

And mother tells the servants that of course
they must contrive
To manage all the household things from four
till half-past five,
For we really cannot suffer interruption from
the cook,
When we cuddle close together with the
happy Fairy-book.

Norman Gale

Grasshopper Green

GRASSHOPPER green is a comical
    chap ;
    He lives on the best of fare.
Bright little trousers, jacket, and cap,
    These are his summer wear.
Out in the meadow he loves to go,
  Playing away in the sun ;
It's hopperty, skipperty, high and low,
  Summer's the time for fun.

Grasshopper green has a quaint little house ;
  It's under the hedge so gay.
Grandmother Spider, as still as a mouse,
  Watches him over the way.
Gladly he's calling the children, I know,
  Out in the beautiful sun ;
It's hopperty, skipperty, high and low,
  Summer's the time for fun.

Unknown

I would like you for a Comrade

I

WOULD like you for a comrade,
    for I love you, that I do,
    I never met a little girl as amiable
    as you ;
I would teach you how to dance and sing, and
    how to talk and laugh,
If I were not a little girl and you were not a
    calf.

II

I would like you for a comrade, you should
    share my barley meal,
And butt me with your little horns just hard
    enough to feel ;
We would lie beneath the chestnut-trees and
    watch the leaves uncurl,
If I were not a clumsy calf and you a little
    girl.

Judge Parry

Little Bell

PIPED the blackbird on the beech-
wood spray,
" Pretty maid, slow wandering this
way,
What's your name?" quoth he—
" What's your name? O stop, and straight
unfold,
Pretty maid with showery curls of gold."—
" Little Bell," said she.

Little Bell gave Each his honest Share ♥

Little Bell sat down beneath the rocks—
Tossed aside her gleaming golden locks—
    " Bonny bird," quoth she,
" Sing me your best song before I go."
" Here's the very finest song I know,
    " Little Bell," said he.

And the blackbird piped ; you never heard
Half so gay a song from any bird ;—
    Full of quips and wiles,
Now so round and rich, now soft and slow,
All for love of that sweet face below,
    Dimpled o'er with smiles.

And the while the bonny bird did pour
His full heart out freely o'er and o'er,
    'Neath the morning skies,
In the little childish heart below,
All the sweetness seemed to grow and grow,
And shine forth in happy overflow
    From the blue, bright eyes.

Down the dell she tripped, and through the
    glade
Peeped the squirrel from the hazel shade,
    And, from out the tree

Swung, and leaped, and frolicked, void of
    fear—
While bold blackbird piped, that all might
    hear,
      " Little Bell ! " piped he.

Little Bell sat down amid the fern :
" Squirrel, squirrel, to your task return—
      Bring me nuts," quoth she.
Up, away the frisky squirrel hies—
Golden wood-lights glancing in his eyes—
      And adown the tree,
Great ripe nuts, kissed brown by July sun,
In the little lap, dropped one by one ;—
Hark, how blackbird pipes to see the fun !
      " Happy Bell ! " pipes he.

Little Bell looked up and down the glade ;
" Squirrel, squirrel, if you're not afraid,
      Come and share with me ! "
Down came the squirrel, eager for his fare,—
Down came bonny blackbird, I declare !
Little Bell gave each his honest share ;
      Ah, the merry three !
                Thomas Westwood

The Violet

DOWN in a green and shady bed
    A modest violet grew ;
Its stalk was bent, it hung its head,
    As if to hide from view.

And yet it was a lovely flower,
    Its colours bright and fair ;
It might have graced a rosy bower,
    Instead of hiding there.

Yet thus it was content to bloom,
    In modest tints arrayed ;
And there diffused a sweet perfume
    Within the silent shade.

Then let me to the valley go,
    This pretty flower to see ;
That I may also learn to grow
    In sweet humility.

Jane Taylor

The Poppy

IGH on a bright and sunny bed
    A scarlet poppy grew ;
And up it held its staring head,
    And thrust it full in view.

Yet no attention did it win,
    By all these efforts made,
And less unwelcome had it been
    In some retired shade.

For though within its scarlet breast
    No sweet perfume was found,
It seemed to think itself the best
    Of all the flowers around.

From this I may a hint obtain,
    And take great care indeed,
Lest I appear as pert and vain
    As does this gaudy weed.

                    Jane Taylor

Robin Redbreast

GOOD-BYE, good-bye to summer !
 For summer's nearly done ;
The garden smiling faintly,
 Cool breezes in the sun ;
Our thrushes now are silent,
 Our swallows flown away,—
But Robin's here in coat of brown,
 With ruddy breast-knot gay.
 Robin, Robin Redbreast,
 O Robin dear !
 Robin singing sweetly
 In the falling of the year.

Bright yellow, red and orange,
 The leaves come down in hosts ;
The trees are Indian Princes,
 But soon they'll turn to Ghosts :
The scanty pears and apples
 Hang russet on the bough,
It's autumn, autumn, autumn late,
 'Twill soon be winter now.
  Robin, Robin Redbreast,
  O Robin dear !
  And weladay ! my Robin,
   For pinching times are near.

The fireside for the cricket,
 The wheatstack for the mouse,
When trembling night-winds whistle
 And moan all round the house ;
The frosty ways like iron,
 The branches plumed with snow,—
Alas ! in winter, dead and dark,
 Where can poor Robin go ?
  Robin, Robin Redbreast,
  O Robin dear !
  And a crumb of bread for Robin,
  His little heart to cheer.

William Allingham

How the Leaves came down

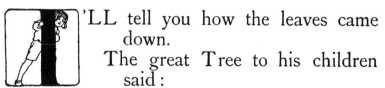

'LL tell you how the leaves came
down.
   The great Tree to his children
said :
" You're getting sleepy, Yellow and Brown,
  Yes, very sleepy, little Red ;
  It is quite time you went to bed."

" Ah," begged each silly pouting leaf,
  " Let us a little longer stay ;
Dear Father Tree, behold our grief ;
  'Tis such a very pleasant day,
  We do not want to go away."

So just for one more merry day
  To the great Tree the leaflets clung,
Frolicked and danced, and had their way,
  Upon the autumn breezes swung,
  Whispering, all their sports among :

" Perhaps, the great Tree will forget,
   And let us stay until the spring,
If we all beg, and coax, and fret."
   But the great Tree did no such thing ;
   He smiled to hear their whispering.

" Come, children all, to bed !" he cried ;
   And ere the leaves could urge their prayer
He shook his head, and far and wide,
   Fluttering and rustling everywhere,
   Down sped the leaflets through the air.

I saw them ; on the ground they lay,
   Golden and red, a huddled swarm,
Waiting, till one from far away,
   White bedclothes heaped upon her arm,
   Should come to wrap them safe and warm.

The great bare Tree looked down, and smiled
   " Good-night, dear little leaves," he said ;
And from below each sleepy child
   Replied, " Good-night," and murmurèd,
   " It is so nice to go to bed."

Susan Coolidge

LITTLE one, come to my knee!
Hark how the rain is pouring
Over the roof, in the pitch-black night,
And the wind in the woods a-roaring!

Hush, my darling, and listen,
　　Then pay for the story with kisses ;
Father was lost in the pitch-black night,
　　In just such a storm as this is !

High up in the lonely mountains,
　　Where the wild men watched and waited :
Wolves in the forest, and bears in the bush,
　　And I on my path belated.

The rain and the night together
　　Came down, and the wind came after,
Bending the props of the pine-tree roof,
　　And snapping many a rafter.

I crept along in the darkness,
　　Stunned and bruised and blinded—
Crept to a fir with thick-set boughs,
　　And a sheltering rock behind it.

There from the blowing and raining,
　　Crouching, I sought to hide me :
Something rustled, two green eyes shone,
　　And a wolf lay down beside me.

Little one, be not frightened :
   I and the wolf together,
Side by side, through the long, long night,
   Hid from the awful weather.

His wet fur pressed against me ;
   Each of us warmed the other ;
Each of us felt, in the stormy dark,
   That beast and man was brother.

And when the falling forest
   No longer crashed in warning,
Each of us went from our hiding-place
   Forth, in the wild wet morning.

Darling, kiss me in payment !
   Hark, how the wind is roaring ;
Father's house is a better place
   When the stormy rain is pouring !

Bayard Taylor

To the Lady-Bird

LADY-BIRD! Lady-bird! fly away
  home;
  The field-mouse is gone to her
  nest,
The daisies have shut up their sleepy red eyes,
  And the birds and the bees are at rest.

Lady-bird! Lady-bird! fly away home;
  The glow-worm is lighting her lamp,
The dew's falling fast, and your fine speckled
  wings
  Will flag with the close-clinging damp.

Lady-bird! Lady-bird! fly away home;
  The fairy-bells tinkle afar;
Make haste, or they'll catch you and harness
  you fast
  With a cobweb to Oberon's car.

Unknown

97

Wynken, Blynken, and Nod.

YNKEN, Blynken, and Nod one
    night
    Sailed off in a wooden shoe—
Sailed on a river of crystal light,
    Into a sea of dew.
"Where are you going, and what do you
    wish?"
    The old moon asked the three.
"We have come to fish for the herring-fish
    That live in this beautiful sea;

Nets of silver and gold have we!"
   Said Wynken, Blynken, and Nod.

The old moon laughed and sang a song,
  As they rocked in the wooden shoe,
And the wind that sped them all night long,
  Ruffled the waves of dew.
The little stars were the herring-fish
  That lived in that beautiful sea—
" Now cast your nets wherever you wish—
  But never afeard are we " ;
So cried the stars to the fishermen three:
  Wynken, Blynken, and Nod.

All night long their nets they threw
  For the fish in the twinkling foam—
Then down from the sky came the wooden
  shoe,
  Bringing the fishermen home ;
'Twas all so pretty a sail, it seemed
  As if it could not be ;
And some folks thought 'twas a dream they'd
  dreamed
  Of sailing that beautiful sea—
But I shall name you the fishermen three:
  Wynken, Blynken, and Nod.

99

Wynken and Blynken are two little eyes,
  And Nod is a little head,
And the wooden shoe that sailed the skies
  Is a wee one's trundle-bed.
So shut your eyes while mother sings
  Of wonderful sights that be,
And you shall see the beautiful things
  As you rock in the misty sea,
  Where the old shoe rocked the fishermen
    three:
    Wynken, Blynken, and Nod.

Eugene Field

From " *With Trumpet and Drum*"; *copyright,*
1892, *by Mary French Field ; published by*
Charles Scribner's Sons and John Lane

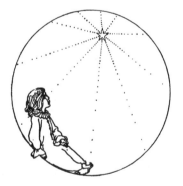

 A Dream

 NCE a dream did weave a shade
O'er my angel-guarded bed,
That an emmet* lost its way
Where on grass methought I lay.

Troubled, wildered, and forlorn,
Dark, benighted, travel-worn,
Over many a tangled spray,
All heart-broke, I heard her say:

" Oh, my children, do they cry,
Do they hear their father sigh?
Now they look abroad to see,
Now return and weep for me."

Pitying, I dropped a tear:
But I saw a glow-worm near,

* *Emmet*, ant.

Who replied, "What wailing wight
Calls the watchman of the night?

"I am set to light the ground,
While the beetle goes his round :
Follow now the beetle's hum ;
Little wanderer, hie thee home!"

William Blake

A Visit from St. Nicolas

'TWAS the night before Christmas,
    when all through the house,
    Not a creature was stirring, not even
    a mouse;
The stockings were hung by the chimney with
    care,
In hopes that St. Nicholas soon would be
    there;
The children were nestled all snug in their
    beds,
While visions of sugar-plums danced in their
    heads;

103

And mamma in her kerchief, and I in my cap,
Had just settled our brains for a long winter's
   nap ;—
When out on the lawn there arose such a
   clatter,
I sprang from my bed to see what was the
   matter.
Away to the window I flew like a flash,
Tore open the shutters and threw up the sash.
The moon on the breast of the new-fallen snow,
Gave the lustre of midday to objects below,
When, what to my wondering eyes should
   appear,
But a miniature sleigh, and eight tiny reindeer,
With a little old driver, so lively and quick,
I knew in a moment it must be St. Nick.
More rapid than eagles his coursers they came,
And he whistled and shouted, and called them
   by name :
" Now, *Dasher!* now, *Dancer!* now, *Prancer!*
   and *Vixen!*
On, *Comet!* on, *Cupid!* on, *Donner* and
   Blitzen!
To the top of the porch! to the top of the
   . wall !
Now dash away ! dash away ! dash away all !"

So up the house-top the Coursers they flew
With the Sleigh full of Toys, and St. Nicolas too.

As dry leaves that before the wild hurricane
  fly,
When they meet with an obstacle, mount to
  the sky;
So up to the house-top the coursers they flew
With the sleigh full of toys, and St. Nicholas
  too.
And then, in a twinkling, I heard on the roof
The prancing and pawing of each little hoof—
As I drew in my head, and was turning around,
Down the chimney St. Nicholas came with a
  bound.
He was dressed all in furs from his head to his
  foot,
And his clothes were all tarnished with ashes
  and soot;
A bundle of toys he had flung on his back,
And he looked like a pedlar just opening his
  pack.
His eyes—how they twinkled! his dimples—
  how merry!
His cheeks were like roses, his nose like a
  cherry!
His droll little mouth was drawn up like a bow,
And the beard on his chin was as white as the
  snow;

The stump of a pipe he held tight in his teeth,
And the smoke it encircled his head like a
wreath ;
He was chubby and plump, a right jolly old
elf ;
And I laughed when I saw him, in spite of
myself ;
A wink of his eye and a twist of his head
Soon gave me to know I had nothing to
dread ;
He spoke not a word, but went straight to his
work,
And filled all the stockings ; then turned with
a jerk,
And laying his finger aside of his nose,
And giving a nod, up the chimney he rose.
He sprang to his sleigh, to his team gave a
whistle,
And away they all flew like the down of a
thistle.
But I heard him exclaim, ere he drove out of
sight,
" *Happy Christmas to all, and to all a good
night !* "

Clement C. Moore

The Willow Man.

THERE once was a Willow, and he was very old,
   And all his leaves fell off from him, and left him in the cold;
But ere the rude winter could buffet him with snow,
There grew upon his hoary head a crop of Mistletoe.

All wrinkled and furrowed was this old Willow's
    skin,
His taper fingers trembled, and his arms were
    very thin ;
Two round eyes and hollow, that stared but
    did not see,
And sprawling feet that never walked, had this
    most ancient tree.

A Dame who dwelt a-near was the only one
    who knew
That every year upon his head the Christmas
    berries grew ;
And when the Dame cut them, she said—it was
    her whim—
" A merry Christmas to you, Sir !" *and left a
bit for him.*

" Oh, Granny dear, tell us," the children cried,
    " where we
May find the shining mistletoe that grows upon
    the tree ? "
At length the Dame told them, but cautioned
    them to mind
To greet the willow civilly, *and leave a bit
behind.*

"Who cares," said the children, "for this old
    Willow-man?
We'll take the Mistletoe, and he may catch us
    if he can."
With rage the ancient Willow shakes in every
    limb,
For they have taken all, and *have not left a bit*
    for him!

Then bright gleamed the holly, the Christmas
    berries shone,
But in the wintry wind without the Willow-man
    did moan:
" Ungrateful, and wasteful! the mystic Mistle-
    toe
A hundred years hath grown on me, but never
    more shall grow."

A year soon passed by, and the children came
    once more,
But not a sprig of Mistletoe the agèd Willow
    bore.
Each slender spray pointed; he mocked them
    in his glee,
And chuckled in his wooden heart, that ancient
    Willow-tree.

MORAL

O children, who gather the spoils of wood and
    wold,
From selfish greed and wilful waste your little
    hands withhold.
Though fair things be common, this moral bear
    in mind,
" Pick thankfully and modestly, *and leave a bit
    behind.*"

Juliana Horatia Ewing

The Spider and the Fly

"WILL you walk into my parlour?"
    said the Spider to the Fly—
    "'Tis the prettiest little parlour
    that ever you did spy;
The way into my parlour is up a winding
    stair,
And I have many curious things to show you
    when you're there."

"Oh, no, no," said the little Fly, "to ask me is
    in vain,
For who goes up your winding stair can ne'er
    come down again."
"I'm sure you must be weary, dear, with soaring
    up so high;
Will you rest upon my little bed?" said the
    Spider to the Fly.
"There are pretty curtains drawn around, the
    sheets are fine and thin,
And if you like to rest a while, I'll snugly tuck
    you in!"
"Oh, no, no," said the little Fly, "for I've often
    heard it said,
They never, never wake again, who sleep upon
    your bed!"

Said the cunning Spider to the Fly: "Dear
    friend, what can I do
To prove the warm affection I've always felt
    for you?
I have, within my pantry, good store of all that's
    nice;
I'm sure you're very welcome—will you please
    to take a slice?"

"Oh, no, no," said the little Fly; "kind sir,
    that cannot be,
I've heard what's in your pantry, and I do not
    wish to see!"
"Sweet creature," said the Spider, "you're
    witty and you're wise;
How handsome are your gauzy wings, how
    brilliant are your eyes!
I have a little looking-glass upon my parlour
    shelf,
If you'll step in one moment, dear, you shall
    behold yourself."
"I thank you, gentle sir," she said, "for what
    you're pleased to say,
And bidding you good-morning now, I'll call
    another day."

The Spider turned him round about, and went
    into his den,
For well he knew the silly Fly would soon come
    back again;
So he wove a subtle web, in a little corner
    sly,
And set his table ready, to dine upon the
    Fly.

Then he came out to his door again, and merrily
    did sing,—
" Come hither, hither, pretty Fly, with the pearl
    and silver wing;
Your robes are green and purple, there's a crest
    upon your head;
Your eyes are like the diamond bright, but
    mine are dull as lead ! "

Alas, alas ! how very soon this silly little
    Fly,
Hearing his wily, flattering words, came slowly
    flitting by :
With buzzing wings she hung aloft, then near
    and nearer drew,—
Thinking only of her brilliant eyes, and green
    and purple hue,
Thinking only of her crested head—poor foolish
    thing ! At last,
Up jumped the cunning Spider, and fiercely
    held her fast ;
He dragged her up his winding stair, into his
    dismal den,
Within his little parlour—but she ne'er came
    out again !

The CHILDREN'S TREASURY

And now, dear little children, who may this
    story read,
To idle, silly, flattering words, I pray you ne'er
    give heed:
Unto an evil counsellor close heart, and ear,
    and eye,
And take a lesson from this tale, of the Spider
    and the Fly.

Mary Howitt

Baby Seed Song

ITTLE brown seed, oh! little
　　brown brother,
　　Are you awake in the dark?
Here we lie cosily, close to each
　　other:
　　Hark to the song of the lark—
"Waken!" the lark says, "waken and dress
　　you,
Put on your green coats and gay;
Blue sky will shine on you, sunshine caress
　　you—
Waken! 'tis morning—'tis May!"

Little brown seed, oh! little brown brother,
  What kind of flower will you be?
I'll be a poppy—all white, like my mother;
  Do be a poppy like me.
What! you're a sun-flower? How I shall miss
   you
  When you're grown golden and high!
But I shall send all the bees up to kiss you;
  Little brown brother, good-bye!

E. Nesbit

The Fairy Folk

COME cuddle close in daddy's coat
　　Beside the fire so bright,
And hear about the fairy folk
　　That wander in the night.
For when the stars are shining clear,
　　And all the world is still,
They float across the silver moon
　　From hill to cloudy hill.

Their caps of red, their cloaks of green,
　　Are hung with silver bells,
And when they're shaken with the wind,
　　Their merry ringing swells.

And riding on the crimson moths
　With black spots on their wings,
They guide them down the purple sky
　With golden bridle rings.

They love to visit girls and boys
　To see how sweet they sleep,
To stand beside their cosy cots
　And at their faces peep.
For in the whole of fairy land
　They have no finer sight
Than little children sleeping sound
　With faces rosy bright.

On tip-toe crowding round their heads,
　When bright the moonlight beams,
They whisper little tender words
　That fill their minds with dreams ;
And when they see a sunny smile,
　With lightest finger tips
They lay a hundred kisses sweet
　Upon the ruddy lips.

And then the little spotted moths
　Spread out their crimson wings,

And bear away the fairy crowd
  With shaking bridle rings.
Come, bairnies, hide in daddy's coat,
  Beside the fire so bright—
Perhaps the little fairy folk
  Will visit you to-night.

Robert M. Bird

Water Jewels

A MILLION little diamonds
    Twinkled on the trees ;
And all the little maidens said,
    " A jewel, if you please ! "

But when they held their hands outstretched
    To catch the diamonds gay,
A million little sunbeams came,
    And stole them all away.

Mary F. Butts

Chanticleer

WAKE! I feel the day is near;
   I hear the red cock crowing!
He cries, "'Tis dawn!" How·sweet
    and clear
His cheerful call comes to my ear,
  While light is slowly growing!

The white snow gathers flake on flake;
   I hear the red cock crowing!
Is anybody else awake
To see the winter morning break,
  While thick and fast 'tis snowing?

I think the world is all asleep;
   I hear the red cock crowing!

Out of the frosty pane I peep ;
The drifts are piled so wide and deep,
  And the wild wind is blowing !

Nothing I see has shape or form ;
  I hear the red cock crowing !
But that dear voice comes through the storm
To greet me in my nest so warm,
  As if the sky were glowing !

A happy little child, I lie
  And hear the red cock crowing.
The day is dark. I wonder why
His voice rings out so brave and high,
  With gladness overflowing.

Celia Thaxter

A SEA-SONG FROM THE SHORE

 AIL! Ho!
  Sail! Ho!
Ahoy! Ahoy! Ahoy!
  Who calls to me,
  So far at sea?
Only a little boy!

125

Sail! Ho!
Hail! Ho!
The sailor he sails the sea :
  I wish he would capture
  A little sea-horse
And send him home to me.

  I wish as he sails
  Through the tropical gales,
He would catch me a sea-bird, too,
  With its silver wings
  And the song it sings,
And its breast of down and dew!

  I wish he would catch me
  A little mermaid,
Some island where he lands,
  With her dripping curls,
  And her crown of pearls,
And the looking-glass in her hands!

  Hail! Ho!
  Sail! Ho!
Sail far o'er the fabulous main!

And if I were a sailor,
I'd sail with you,
Though I never sailed back again.

James   Whitcomb   Riley

Mustard and Cress

LIZABETH, my cousin, is the sweetest little girl,
From her eyes, like dark blue pansies, to her tiniest golden curl;
    I do not use her great long name, but simply call her Bess,
And yesterday I planted her in mustard and in cress.

My garden is so narrow that there's very little room,
But I'd rather have her name than get a hollyhock to bloom;
And before she comes to visit us with Charley and with Jess,
She'll pop up green and bonny out of mustard and of cress.

Norman Gale

Waking Up ♡ ♡

MILLIONS of cradles up in the
    trees
Rock to and fro in the gentle
    breeze;
Tucked in these bud-cradles snug and warm
The little green leaves sleep, safe from harm.

April sings low as she passes by,
" Dear little leaves, the summer is nigh;
Open your eyes, from your cradles creep,
Wake up, little leaves, wake up from sleep!"

Millions of leaves from their cradle-beds
Slowly and timidly raise their heads;

They see the sun, and they love it so
They back no more to their cradles go.

Stronger and stronger they grow each hour,
Bathing in sunshine and soft spring shower ;
They stretch themselves out on every side,
Saying, " Dear me ! but this world is wide."

They gaze and gaze on the deep blue sky,
They watch the white clouds go sailing by,
The winds sing songs till for very glee
The leaves are dancing on every tree.

From "Nature Study and the Child"

All Things Bright and Beautiful.

 ALL things bright and beautiful,
　　All creatures great and small
All things wise and wonderful,
　　The Lord God made them all.

Each little flower that opens,
　　Each little bird that sings,

He made their glowing colours,
   He made their tiny wings.

The purple-headed mountain,
   The river running by,
The sunset and the morning
   That brightens up the sky.

The cold wind in the winter,
   The pleasant summer sun,
The ripe fruits in the garden,
   He made them every one.

The tall trees in the greenwood,
   The meadows where we play,
The rushes by the water,
   We gather every day ;—

He gave us eyes to see them,
   And lips that we might tell
How great is God Almighty,
   Who has made all things well.

          C. Frances Alexander

The Brown Thrush

THERE'S a merry brown thrush sitting up in the tree;
"He's singing to me! he's singing to me!"
And what does he say, little girl, little boy?
"Oh, the world's running over with joy!
  Don't you hear? Don't you see?
  Hush! look! in my tree!
  I'm as happy as happy can be!"

And the brown thrush keeps singing, " A nest
do you see,
And five eggs hid by me in the juniper-
tree?
Don't meddle! don't touch! little girl, little
boy,
Or the world will lose some of its joy!
　　Now I'm glad! now I'm free!
　　And I always shall be,
　　If you never bring sorrow to me."

So the merry brown thrush sings away in the
tree,
To you and to me, to you and to me;
And he sings all the day, little girl, little
boy,
" Oh, the world's running over with joy!
　　But long it won't be,
　　Don't you know? don't you see?
　　Unless we are as good as can be!"

Lucy Larcom

The Lamplighter

Y tea is nearly ready, and the sun has
      left the sky ;
It's time to take the window to see
      Leerie going by ;
For every night at tea-time and before you take
      your seat,
With lantern and with ladder he comes posting
      up the street.

136

Now Tom would be a driver and Maria go to
    sea,
And my papa's a banker and as rich as he
    can be ;
But I, when I am stronger and can choose what
    I'm to do,
O Leerie, I'll go round at night and light the
    lamps with you !

For we are very lucky, with a lamp before the
    door,
And Leerie stops to light it as he lights so
    many more ;
And O ! before you hurry by with ladder and
    with light,
O Leerie, see a little child and nod to him
    to-night !

Robert Louis Stevenson

THE PEDLAR'S CARAVAN

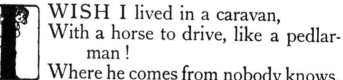

I WISH I lived in a caravan,
With a horse to drive, like a pedlar-
man !
Where he comes from nobody knows,
Or where he goes to, but on he goes !

His caravan has windows two,
And a chimney of tin, that the smoke comes
through ;
He has a wife, with a baby brown,
And they go riding from town to town.

Chairs to mend, and delf to sell !
He clashes the basins like a bell ;
Tea-trays, baskets ranged in order,
Plates with the alphabet round the border !

The roads are brown, and the sea is green,
But his house is like a bathing-machine ;
The world is round, and he can ride,
Rumble and splash to the other side !

With the pedlar-man I should like to roam,
And write a book when I came home ;
All the people would read my book,
Just like the Travels of Captain Cook !

William Brighty Rands

The Bird in a Cage

OH! who would keep a little bird
    confined?
When cowslip-bells are nodding in
    the wind,
When every hedge as with "Good-morrow"
    rings,
And, heard from wood to coombe, the black-
    bird sings.
Oh! who would keep a little bird confined
In his cold, wiry prison?—Let him fly,
And hear him sing, "How sweet is liberty!"

William Lisle Bowles

Seven Times One

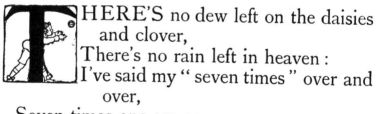HERE'S no dew left on the daisies
    and clover,
There's no rain left in heaven :
I've said my " seven times " over and
    over,
Seven times one are seven.

I am old, so old, I can write a letter ;
  My birthday lessons are done ;

The lambs play always, they know no better ;
  They are only one times one.

O moon ! in the night I have seen you
      sailing
  And shining so round and low ;
You were bright ! ah, bright ! but your light
      is failing—
You are nothing now but a bow.

You moon, have you done something wrong
      in heaven
  That God has hidden your face ?
I hope if you have you will soon be for-
      given,
  And shine again in your place.

O velvet bee, you're a dusty fellow,
  You've powdered your legs with gold !
O brave marsh marybuds, rich and yellow,
  Give me your money to hold !

O columbine, open your folded wrapper,
  Where two twin turtle-doves dwell !
O cuckoopint, toll me the purple clapper
  That hangs in your clear, green bell !

And show me your nest with the young ones
    in it ;
  I will not steal them away ;
I am old ! you may trust me, linnet, linnet—
  I am seven times one to-day.

Jean Ingelow

Pretty Cow

THANK you, pretty cow, that made
Pleasant milk to soak my bread,
Every day and every night,
Warm, and fresh, and sweet, and
white.

Do not chew the hemlock rank,
Growing on the weedy bank ;
But the yellow cowslip eat,
That will make it very sweet.

Where the purple violet grows,
Where the bubbling water flows,
Where the grass is fresh and fine,
Pretty cow, go there and dine.

Jane Taylor

Discontent

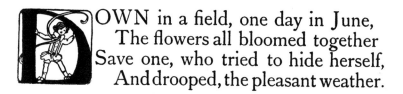 OWN in a field, one day in June,
   The flowers all bloomed together
Save one, who tried to hide herself,
   And drooped, the pleasant weather.

A robin who had flown too high
   And felt a little lazy,
Was resting near this buttercup,
   Who wished she were a daisy.

For daisies grow so smart and tall ;
   She always had a passion

For wearing frills around her neck,
  In just the daisies' fashion.

And buttercups must always be
  The same old tiresome colour,
While daisies dress in gold and white,
  Although their gold is duller.

" Dear robin," said this sad young flower,
  " Perhaps you'd not mind trying
To find a nice white frill for me,
  Some day when you are flying ? "

" You silly thing ! " the robin said,
  " I think you must be crazy ;
I'd rather be my honest self
  Than any made-up daisy.

" You're nicer in your own bright gown,
  The little children love you.
Be the best buttercup you can,
  And think no flower above you.

" Though swallows leave me out of sight,
  We'd better keep our places ;
Perhaps the world would all go wrong
  With one too many daisies.

" Look bravely up into the sky,
   And be content with knowing
That God wished for a buttercup
   Just here, where you are growing."
                    Sarah Orne Jewett

The LARK'S GRAVE

WE'LL plant a corn-flower on his grave,
  And a grain of the bearded barley,
And a little bluebell to ring his knell,
 And eye-bright, blossoming early;
  And we'll cover it over,
  With purple clover,
And daisies, crimson and pearly.

149

And we'll pray the linnet to chant his dirge,
  With the robin and wren for chorus ;
His mate, on high, shall rain from the sky
  Her benedictions o'er us ;
    And the hawk and owls,
    Those pitiless fowls,
  We'll drive away before us.

And then we'll leave him to his rest,
  And whisper soft above him,
That ever his song was sweet and strong,
  Nor cloud nor mist could move him ;
    In his strain was a gladness
    To cure all sadness,
  And all fair things did love him.

                              Thomas Westwood

BIRDS' NESTS

HE skylark's nest among the grass
And waving corn is found ;
The robin's on a shady bank,
With oak leaves strewn around.

The wren builds in an ivied thorn,
Or old and ruined wall ;
The mossy nest, so covered in,
You scarce can see at all.

The martins build their nests of clay,
  In rows beneath the eaves ;
While silvery lichens, moss, and hair,
  The chaffinch interweaves.

The cuckoo makes no nest at all,
  But through the wood she strays
Until she finds one snug and warm,
  And there her eggs she lays.

The sparrow has a nest of hay,
  With feathers warmly lined ;
The ring-dove's careless nest of sticks
  On lofty trees we find.

Rooks build together in a wood,
  And often disagree ;
The owl will build inside a barn
  Or in a hollow tree.

The blackbird's nest of grass and mud
  In brush and bank is found ;
The lapwing's darkly spotted eggs
  Are laid upon the ground.

The magpie's nest is girt with thorns
   In leafless tree or hedge ;
The wild duck and the water hen
   Build by the water's edge.

Birds build their nests from year to year,
   According to their kind,—
Some very neat and beautiful,
   Some easily designed.

The habits of each little bird,
   And all its patient skill,
Are surely taught by God Himself
   And ordered by His will.

                       Unknown

·Trees

 HE Oak is called the King of
　　Trees,
　　The Aspen quivers in the breeze,
　　The Poplar grows up straight and
　　　　tall,
The Pear-tree spreads along the wall,

The CHILDREN'S TREASURY

The Sycamore gives pleasant shade,
The Willow droops in watery glade,
The Fir-tree useful timber gives,
The Beech amid the forest lives.

Sara Coleridge

The Owl and the Pussy-Cat

HE Owl and the Pussy-Cat went
to sea
In a beautiful pea-green boat,
They took some honey, and plenty
of money,
Wrapped up in a five-pound note.

The Owl looked up to the stars above,
  And sang to a small guitar,
"O lovely Pussy! O Pussy, my love,
  What a beautiful Pussy you are,
          You are!
  What a beautiful Pussy you are!"

Pussy said to the Owl, "You elegant fowl!
  How charmingly sweet you sing!
O let us be married! too long we have tar-
  ried:
  But what shall we do for a ring?"
They sailed away for a year and a day,
  To the land where the Bong-tree grows,
And there in a wood a Piggy-wig stood,
  With a ring at the end of his nose,
          His nose,
  With a ring at the end of his nose.

"Dear Pig, are you willing to sell for one shil-
  ling
  Your ring?"   Said the Piggy, "I will."
So they took it away, and were married next
  day
  By the Turkey who lives on the hill.

They dinèd on mince and slices of quince,
    Which they ate with a runcible spoon ;
And hand in hand, on the edge of the sand,
    They danced by the light of the moon,
            The moon,
They danced by the light of the moon.

Edward Lear

BIG SMITH

RE you a Giant, great big man, or
   is your real name Smith?
   Nurse says you've got a hammer
      that you hit bad children with.
I'm good to-day, and so I've come to see if it
   is true
That you can turn a red-hot rod into a horse's
   shoe.

Why do you make the horses' shoes of iron
    instead of leather ?
Is it because they are allowed to go out in
    bad weather ?
If horses should be shod with iron, Big Smith,
    will you shoe mine ?
For now I may not take him out, excepting
    when it's fine.

Although he's not a real live horse, I'm very
    fond of him ;
His harness won't take off and on, but still it's
    new and trim.
His tail is hair, he has four legs, but neither
    hoofs nor heels;
I think he'd seem more like a horse without
    these yellow wheels.

They say that Dapple-grey's not yours, but don't
    you wish he were ?
My horse's coat is only paint, but his is soft grey
    hair ;
His face is big and kind like yours, his forelock
    white as snow—
Shan't you be sorry when you've done his shoes
    and he must go?

I do so wish, Big Smith, that I might come and
    live with you;
To rake the fire, to heat the rods, to hammer
    two and two.
To be so black, and not to have to wash unless
    I choose;
To pat the dear old horses, and to mend their
    poor old shoes!

When all the world is dark at night, you work
    among the stars,
A shining shower of fireworks beat out of red-
    hot bars.
I've seen you beat, I've heard you sing, when I
    was going to bed;
And now your face and arms looked black, and
    now were glowing red.

The more you work, the more you sing, the
    more the bellows roar;
The falling stars, the flying sparks, stream
    shining more and more.
You hit so hard, you look so hot, and yet you
    never tire;
It must be very nice to be allowed to play with
    fire.

I long to beat and sing and shine, as you do,
but instead
I put away my horse, and Nurse puts me away
to bed.
I wonder if you go to bed; I often think I'll
keep
Awake and see, but, though I try, I always
fall asleep.

I know it's very silly, but I sometimes am
afraid
Of being in the dark alone, especially in bed.
But when I see your forge-light come and go
upon the wall,
And hear you through the window, I am not
afraid at all.

I often hear a trotting horse, I sometimes hear
it stop;
I hold my breath—you stay your song—it's at
the blacksmith's shop.
Before it goes, I'm apt to fall asleep, Big Smith,
it's true;
But then I dream of hammering that horse's
shoes with you!

Juliana Horatia Ewing

The FAIRIES

UP the airy mountain,
 Down the rushy glen,
We daren't go a-hunting,
 For fear of little men ;

Wee folk, good folk,
    Trooping all together ;
Green jacket, red cap,
    And white owl's feather !

Down along the rocky shore
    Some make their home,
They live on crispy pancakes
    Of yellow tide-foam ;
Some in the reeds
    Of the black mountain lake,
With frogs for their watch-dogs,
    All night awake.

High on the hill-top
    The old King sits ;
He is now so old and gray,
    He's nigh lost his wits.
With a bridge of white mist
    Columbkill he crosses
On his stately journeys
    From Slieveleague to Rosses ;
Or going up with music
    On cold, starry nights,
To sup with the Queen
    Of the gay Northern Lights.

They stole little Bridget
   For seven years long ;
When she came down again,
   Her friends were all gone.
They took her lightly back,
   Between the night and morrow,
They thought that she was fast asleep,
   But she was dead with sorrow.
They have kept her ever since
   Deep within the lake,
On a bed of flag leaves,
   Watching till she wake.

By the craggy hill-side,
   Through the mosses bare,
They have planted thorn-trees
   For pleasure here and there.
Is any man so daring
   As dig them up in spite,
He shall find their sharpest thorns
   In his bed at night.

Up the airy mountain,
   Down the rushy glen,
We daren't go a-hunting
   For fear of little men;

The CHILDREN'S TREASURY

Wee folk, good folk,
   Trooping all together ;
Green jacket, red cap,
   And white owl's feather !

William Allingham

Answer to a Child's Question

 DO you ask what the birds say? The
sparrow, the dove,
The linnet and thrush say, "I love
and I love!"
In the winter they're silent—the wind is so
strong;   [song.
What it says, I don't know, but it sings a loud
But green leaves and blossoms and sunny
warm weather,
And singing and loving — all come back
together.
But the lark is so brimful of gladness and love,
The green fields below him, the blue sky
above,
That he sings, and he sings; and for ever
sings he—
"I love my Love, and my Love loves me!"

Samuel Taylor Coleridge

JOG ON, JOG ON

 OG on, jog on, the footpath way,
　　And merrily hent the style-a:
A merry heart goes all the day,
　　Your sad tires in a mile-a.

William Shakespeare

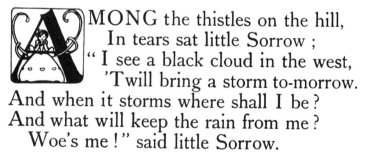

Little Sorrow

AMONG the thistles on the hill,
　　In tears sat little Sorrow ;
" I see a black cloud in the west,
　　'Twill bring a storm to-morrow.
And when it storms where shall I be ?
And what will keep the rain from me ?
　　Woe's me !" said little Sorrow.

" But now the air is soft and sweet,
  The sun is bright," said Pleasure ;
" Here is my pipe ; if you will dance,
  I'll wake my merriest measure ;
Or, if you choose, we'll sit beneath
The red rose-tree, and twine a wreath ;
  Come, come with me !" said Pleasure.

" O, I want neither dance nor flowers,—
  They're not for me," said Sorrow,
" When that black cloud is in the west,
  And it will storm to-morrow !
And if it storm what shall I do ?
I have no heart to play with you,—
  Go ! go !" said little Sorrow.

But, lo ! when came the morrow's morn,
  The clouds were all blown over ;
The lark sprang singing from his nest
  Among the dewy clover ;
And Pleasure called, " Come out and dance !
To-day you mourn no evil chance ;
  The clouds have all blown over !"

" And if they have, alas ! alas !
  Poor comfort that !" said Sorrow ;

" For if to-day we miss the storm,
   'Twill surely come to-morrow,—
And be the fiercer for delay !
I am too sore at heart to play ;
   Woe's me !" said little Sorrow.

Marian Douglas

SUPPOSE

SUPPOSE the little cowslip
    Should hang its golden cup,
And say, " I'm such a tiny flower,
    I'd better not grow up!"
How many a weary traveller
    Would miss its fragrant smell!
How many a little child would grieve
    To miss it from the dell!

Suppose the glistening dewdrop
    Upon the grass should say,
" What can a little dewdrop do?
    I'd better roll away ";

The blade on which it rested,
   Before the day was done,
Without a drop to moisten it,
   Would wither in the sun.

Suppose the little breezes
   Upon a summer's day,
Should think themselves too small to cool
   The traveller on his way ;
Who would not miss the smallest
   And softest ones that blow,
And think they made a great mistake
   If they were talking so ?

How many deeds of kindness
   A little child may do,
Although it has so little strength,
   And little wisdom too ?
It wants a loving spirit
   Much more than strength, to prove
How many things a child may do
   For others by its love.

Fanny van Alstyne

Lullaby

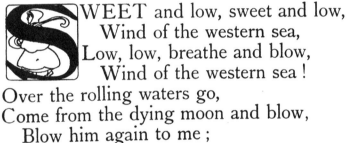

SWEET and low, sweet and low,
    Wind of the western sea,
Low, low, breathe and blow,
    Wind of the western sea !
Over the rolling waters go,
Come from the dying moon and blow,
  Blow him again to me ;
While my little one, while my pretty one,
    sleeps.

Sleep and rest, sleep and rest,
  Father will come to thee soon ;
Rest, rest, on mother's breast,
  Father will come to thee soon ;

Father will come to his babe in the nest,
Silver sails all out of the west
   Under the silver moon :
Sleep, my little one ; sleep, my pretty one,
   sleep.

Lord Tennyson

Cradle Song

WHAT does little birdie say
In her nest at peep of day?
Let me fly, says little birdie,
Mother, let me fly away.
Birdie, rest a little longer,
Till the little wings are stronger.
So she rests a little longer,
Then she flies away.

What does little baby say,
In her bed at peep of day?
Baby says, like little birdie,
Let me rise and fly away.
Baby, sleep a little longer,
Till the little limbs are stronger.
If she sleeps a little longer,
Baby too shall fly away.

Lord Tennyson

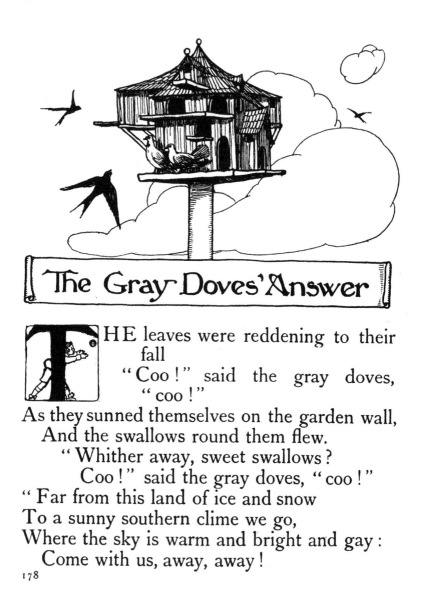

The Gray Doves' Answer

THE leaves were reddening to their
     fall
     "Coo!" said the gray doves,
       "coo!"
As they sunned themselves on the garden wall,
  And the swallows round them flew.
    "Whither away, sweet swallows?
      Coo!" said the gray doves, "coo!"
"Far from this land of ice and snow
To a sunny southern clime we go,
Where the sky is warm and bright and gay:
  Come with us, away, away!

" Come," they said, " to that sunny clime ! "
 " Coo ! " said the gray doves, " coo ! "
" You will die in this land of mist and rime,
 Where 'tis bleak the winter through.
 Come away ! " said the swallows.
 " Coo ! " said the gray doves, " coo !
Oh, God in heaven," they said, " is good ;
And little hands will give us food,
And guard us all the winter through.
 Coo ! " said the gray doves, " coo ! "

Fred. E. Weatherly

How the little Kite learned to fly

"I NEVER can do it," the little kite said,
As he looked at the others high
over his head;
"I know I should fall if I tried to fly."
"Try," said the big kite; "only try!
Or I fear you never will learn at all."
But the little kite said, "I'm afraid I'll fall."

The big kite nodded: "Ah, well, good-bye;
I'm off"; and he rose toward the tranquil sky.
Then the little kite's paper stirred at the sight,
And trembling he shook himself free for flight.
First whirling and frightened, then braver
grown,
Up, up he rose through the air alone,

180

Till the big kite looking down could see
The little one rising steadily.

Then how the little kite thrilled with pride,
As he sailed with the big kite side by side!
While far below he could see the ground,
And the boys like small spots moving round.
They rested high in the quiet air,
And only the birds and clouds were there.
"Oh, how happy I am!" the little kite cried;
"And all because I was brave, and tried."

Unknown

LITTLE ♡ ♡ GOTTLIEB

A Christmas
. . Story . .

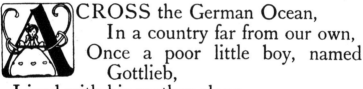

ACROSS the German Ocean,
   In a country far from our own,
Once a poor little boy, named
      Gottlieb,
Lived with his mother alone.

He was not large enough to work,
   And his mother could do no more
(Though she scarcely laid her knitting down)
   Than keep the wolf from the door.

She had to take their threadbare clothes,
   And turn, and patch, and darn ;

For never any woman yet
  Grew rich by knitting yarn.

And oft at night, beside her chair,
  Would Gottlieb sit, and plan
The wonderful things he would do for her,
  When he grew to be a man.

One night she sat and knitted,
  And Gottlieb sat and dreamed,
When a happy fancy all at once
  Upon his vision beamed.

'Twas only a week till Christmas
  And Gottlieb knew that then
The Christ-Child, who was born that day,
  Sent down good gifts to men.

But he said, " He will never find us,
  Our home is so mean and small ;
And we, who have most need of them,
  Will get no gifts at all."

When all at once a happy light
  Came into his eyes so blue,
And lighted up his face with smiles,
  As he thought what he could do.

Next day when the postman's letters
  Came from all over the land,
Came one for the Christ-Child, written
  In a child's poor trembling hand.

You may think the postman was troubled
  What in the world to do ;
So he went to the Burgomaster,
  As the wisest man he knew.

And when they opened the letter,
  They stood almost dismayed
That such a little child should dare
  To ask the Lord for aid.

Then the Burgomaster stammered
  And scarce knew what to speak,
And hastily he brushed aside
  A drop, like a tear, from his cheek.

Then up he spake right gruffly,
  And turned himself about :
" This must be a very foolish boy,
  And a small one, too, no doubt."

A wise and learned man was he,
  Men called him good and just ;

But his wisdom seemed like foolishness
  By that weak child's simple trust.

Now when the morn of Christmas came
  And the long, long week was done,
Poor Gottlieb, who could scarcely sleep,
  Rose up before the sun,

And hastened to his mother,
  But he scarce might speak for fear,
When he saw her wondering look, and saw
  The Burgomaster near.

Amazed the poor child looked, to find
  The hearth was piled with wood,
And the table, never full before,
  Was heaped with dainty food.

Then half to hide from himself the truth
  The Burgomaster said,
While the mother blessed him on her knees,
  And Gottlieb shook for dread:

" Nay, give no thanks, my worthy dame,
  To such as me for aid,
Be grateful to your little son,
  And the Lord to whom he prayed!"

Then turning round to Gottlieb,
  "Your written prayer, you see,
Came not to Whom it was addressed,
  It only came to me!

"'Twas but a foolish thing you did,
  As you must understand;
For though the gifts are yours, you know,
  You have them from my hand."

Then Gottlieb answered fearlessly,
  Where he humbly stood apart,
"But the Christ-Child sent them all the
    same,
He put the thought in your heart!"

Phœbe Cary

A Prayer

FATHER, we thank Thee for the
night
And for the pleasant morning light,
For rest and food and loving care,
And all that makes the world so fair.
Help us to do the thing we should,
To be to others kind and good,
In all we do, in all we say,
To grow more loving every day.

Unknown

THE FOUR SUNBEAMS

OUR little sunbeams came earth-
ward one day,
All shining and dancing along on
their way,
Resolved that their course should be blest.

"Let us try," they all whispered, "some kind-
ness to do,
Not seek our own happiness all the day through,
Then meet at eve in the west."

One sunbeam ran in at a low cottage door,
And played hide-and-seek with a child on the
floor,
Till baby laughed loud in his glee,
And chased in delight his strange playmate so
bright,
The little hands grasping in vain for the light
That ever before them would flee.

One crept to the couch where an invalid lay,
And brought him a dream of the sweet sum-
mer day,
Its bird-song and beauty and bloom ;
Till pain was forgotten, and weary unrest,
And in fancy he roamed through the scenes he
loved best,
Far away from the dim, darkened room.

One stole to the heart of a flower that was sad,
And loved and caressed her until she was glad,
And lifted her white face again ;

For love brings content to the lowliest lot,
And finds something sweet in the dreariest
spot,
  And lightens all labour and pain.

And one, where a little blind girl sat alone,
Not sharing the mirth of her playfellows, shone
  On hands that were folded and pale,
And kissed the poor eyes that had never known
sight,
That never would gaze on the beautiful light,
  Till angels had lifted the veil.

At last, when the shadows of evening were
falling,
And the Sun, their great father, his children
was calling,
  Four sunbeams passed into the west.
All said, "We have found that in seeking the
pleasure
Of others we fill to the full our own measure,"—
  Then softly they sank to their rest.

M. K. B.

The Bee and the Lily

"**B**UZZ!**" went the Bee, with a
        merry din.
        "Who's there?" cried the Lily,
        her cup within.
"Your gossip, the Bee, with a tale *so* funny,
To hum in your ear while you brew your
        honey;
But you must not repeat it, for love or money!"
"Buzz!" went the rogue, with a merry din,
As the Lily opened and let him in.

193

"Why, Lily, I vow it's a palace quite,
This kitchen of yours, so warm and white,
And such fine honey!—Now, might I venture
To sniff, for a moment, to . . . taste, to sip
A morsel, merely to moisten my lip,
Without incurring thereby your censure?"
"Oh," said the Lily, "pray eat your fill."
So the Bee set to work with a right good will;
He fluttered and buzzed, he tried and tasted;
Nothing was missed and nothing wasted;
He ate and he ate—it was really funny
To see him swallow such heaps of honey.
He swallowed it *all;* and, when cups and
 platters,
And saucers and jars, and other matters,
Were emptied at last, and not a drop
Remained,—"Well, now," said the Lily,
 "stop,
And be sober and steady, my gossip dear,
While you whisper, cosily, in my ear,
That tale you promised so rare and new."
"Buzz!" said the Bee, and away he flew.

      Thomas Westwood

Prince Tatters

ITTLE Prince Tatters has lost
     his cap!
   Over the hedge he threw it;
Into the water it fell with a clap—
Stupid old thing to do it!
Now Mother may sigh and Nurse may fume
For the gay little cap with its eagle plume.
"One cannot be thinking all day of such
     matters.
Trifles are trifles!" says little Prince Tatters.

Little Prince Tatters has lost his coat!
  Playing, he did not need it;
" Left it *right there*, by the nanny-goat,
  And nobody ever see'd it!"
Now Mother and Nurse may search till night
For the new little coat with its buttons bright;
But, "Coat-sleeves or shirt-sleeves, how little it
    matters!
Trifles are trifles!" says little Prince Tatters.

Little Prince Tatters has LOST HIS BALL!
  Rolled away down the street!
Somebody'll *have to find it*, that's all,
  Before he can sleep or eat.

196

Now raise the neighbourhood, quickly,
   do !
And send for the crier and constable
   too !
" Trifles are trifles ; but serious
   matters,
They must be *seen to*," says Little
   Prince Tatters.

Laura E. Richards

THE ☆ FROST

THE Frost looked forth one still, clear night
 And whispered, "Now I shall be out of sight;
So through the valley and over the height
 In silence I'll take my way.
I will not go on like that blustering train—
The wind and the snow, the hail and the rain—
Who make so much bustle and noise in vain;
 But I'll be as busy as they."

198

Then he flew to the mountain and powdered
 its crest,
He lit on the trees and their boughs he dressed
With diamond beads ; and over the breast
 Of the quivering lake he spread
A coat of mail, that it need not fear
The downward point of many a spear
That he hung on its margin, far and near,
 Where a rock could rear its head.

He went to the windows of those who slept,
And over each pane, like a fairy, crept ;
Wherever he breathed, wherever he stept,
 By the light of the morn were seen
Most beautiful things ; there were flowers and
 trees,
There were bevies of birds and swarms of
 bees ;
There were cities and temples and towers; and
 these
 All pictured in silver sheen.
But he did one thing that was hardly fair ;
He went to the cupboard, and finding there
That all had forgotten for him to prepare—
 " Now just to set them a-thinking,

I'll bite this basket of fruit," said he,
" This costly pitcher I'll burst in three ;
And the glass of water they have left for me
    Shall 'tchick!' to tell them I'm drinking."

Hannah Flagg Gould

OTHING is quite so quiet and clean
  As snow that falls in the night;
And isn't it jolly to jump from bed
And find the whole world white?

It lies on the window ledges,
  It lies on the boughs of the trees,
While sparrows crowd at the kitchen door,
  With a pitiful " If you *please !*"

It lies on the arm of the lamp-post,
　　Where the lighter's ladder goes,
And the policeman under it beats his arms,
　　And stamps—to feel his toes ;

The butcher's boy is rolling a ball
　　To throw at the man with coals,
And old Mrs. Ingram has fastened a piece
　　Of flannel under her soles ;

No sound there is in the snowy road
　　From the horses' cautious feet,
And all is hushed but the postman's knocks
　　Rat-tatting down the street,

Till the men come round with shovels
　　To clear the snow away,—
What a pity it is that when it falls
　　They never let it stay !

Rickman Mark

The Wood~Mouse

O ye know the little wood-mouse,
  That pretty little thing,
That sits amongst the forest leaves,
  Beside the forest spring?

Its fur is red as the chestnut,
  And it is small and slim,
It leads a life most innocent
  Within the forest dim.

'Tis a timid, gentle creature,
  And seldom comes in sight ;
It has a long and wiry tail,
  And eyes both black and bright.

It makes its nest of soft, dry moss,
  In a hole so deep and strong;
And there it sleeps secure and warm,
  The dreary winter long.

And though it keeps no calendar
  It knows when flowers are springing ;
And waketh to its summer life
  When nightingales are singing.

Upon the bough the squirrel sits,
  The wood-mouse plays below;
And plenty of food it finds itself
  Where the beech and chestnut grow.

In the hedge-sparrow's nest it sits,
  When the summer brood is fled,
And picks the berries from the bough
  Of the hawthorn overhead.

I saw a little wood-mouse once,
   Like Oberon in his hall,
With the green, green moss beneath his
     feet,
   Sit under a mushroom tall.

I saw him sit and his dinner eat,
   All under the forest tree—
His dinner of chestnut ripe and red,
   And he ate it heartily.

I wish you could have seen him there:
   It did my spirit good,
To see the small thing God had made,
   Thus eating in the wood.

I saw that He regardeth them,
   Those creatures weak and small,
Their table in the wild is spread
   By Him who cares for all!

                  Mary Howitt

Lullaby of an Infant Chief

 HUSH thee, my babie, thy sire was
a knight,
Thy mother a lady, both lovely and
bright ;
The woods and the glens, from the towers
which we see,
They all are belonging, dear babie, to thee.

O, fear not the bugle, though loudly it blows,
It calls but the warders that guard thy repose ;

Their bows would be bended, their blades would
be red,
Ere the step of a foeman drew near to thy bed.

O, hush thee, my babie, the time soon will
come
When thy sleep shall be broken by trumpet and
drum ;
Then hush thee, my darling, take rest while you
may,
For strife comes with manhood, and waking
with day.

Sir Walter Scott

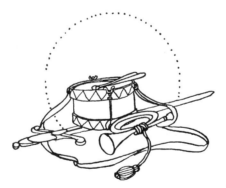

Among the Nuts

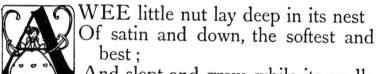

WEE little nut lay deep in its nest
Of satin and down, the softest and
   best ;
   And slept and grew, while its cradle
      rocked,
As it hung in the boughs that interlocked.

Now the house was small where the cradle
      lay,
As it swung in the wind by night and day ;
For a thicket of underbrush fenced it round,
This little lone cot by the great sun browned.

The little nut grew, and ere long it found
There was work outside on the soft green
    ground;
It must do its part so the world might know
It had tried one little seed to sow.

And soon the house that had kept it warm
Was tossed about by the winter's storm;
The stem was cracked, the old house fell,
And the chestnut burr was an empty shell.

But the little seed, as it waiting lay,
Dreamed a wonderful dream from day to day,
Of how it should break its coat of brown,
And live as a tree to grow up and down.

From " Nature Study and the Child"

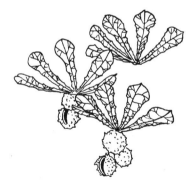

A FRIEND IN THE GARDEN

HE is not John the gardener,
    And yet the whole day long
Employs himself most usefully
    The flower-beds among.

He is not Tom the pussy-cat;
    And yet the other day,
With stealthy stride and glistening eye,
    He crept upon his prey.

He is not Dash, the dear old dog,
    And yet, perhaps, if you
Took pains with him and petted him,
    You'd come to love him too.

He's not a blackbird, though he chirps,
　　And though he once was black;
And now he wears a loose, grey coat,
　　All wrinkled on the back.

He's got a very dirty face,
　　And very shining eyes!
He sometimes comes and sits indoors;
　　He looks—and p'r'aps is—wise.

But in a sunny flower-bed
　　He has his fixed abode;
He eats the things that eat my plants—
　　He is a friendly TOAD.

Juliana Horatia Ewing

Queen Mab

 LITTLE fairy comes at night,
　　Her eyes are blue, her hair is
　　　　brown
　　With silver spots upon her wings,
And from the moon she flutters down.

She has a little silver wand,
　　And when a good child goes to bed
She waves her hand from right to left,
　　And makes a circle round its head.

·pretty dwarfs to show tho way·

And then it dreams of pleasant things,
  Of fountains filled with fairy fish,
And trees that bear delicious fruit,
  And bow their branches at a wish:

Of arbours filled with dainty scents
  From lovely flowers that never fade;
Bright flies that glitter in the sun,
  And glow-worms shining in the shade;

And talking birds with gifted tongues
  For singing songs and telling tales,
And pretty dwarfs to show the way
  Through fairy hills and fairy dales.

But when a bad child goes to bed,
  From left to right she weaves her rings,
And then it dreams all through the night
  Of only ugly horrid things!

Then lions come with glaring eyes,
  And tigers growl, a dreadful noise,
And ogres draw their cruel knives,
  To shed the blood of girls and boys.

Then stormy waves rush on to drown,
   Or raging flames come scorching round,
Fierce dragons hover in the air,
   And serpents crawl along the ground.

Then wicked children wake and weep,
   And wish the long black gloom away ;
But good ones love the dark, and find
   The night as pleasant as the day.

Thomas Hood

THE SHEPHERD

HOW sweet is the shepherd's
sweet lot:
From the morn to the evening he strays;
He shall follow his sheep all the day,
And his tongue shall be fillèd with praise.

For he hears the lambs' innocent call,
And he hears the ewes' tender reply;
He is watchful while they are in peace,
For they know when their shepherd is
nigh. *William Blake*

The Lamb

LITTLE lamb, who made thee?
Dost thou know who made thee,
Gave thee life, and bade thee feed
By the stream and o'er the mead;
Gave thee clothing of delight,
Softest clothing, woolly, bright;
Gave thee such a tender voice,
Making all the vales rejoice?
Little lamb, who made thee?
Dost thou know who made thee?

Little lamb, I'll tell thee ;
Little lamb, I'll tell thee ;
He is callèd by thy name,
For He calls Himself a lamb ;
He is meek and He is mild,
He became a little child.
I a child and thou a lamb,
We are callèd by His name.
Little lamb, God bless thee !
Little lamb, God bless thee !

William Blake

The Sea Princess

In a palace of pearl and sea-weed
set round with shining shells,
Under the deeps of the ocean,
the little sea princess dwells.

Sometimes she sees the shadows
  Of great whales passing by,
Or white-winged vessels sailing
  Between the sea and sky.

And when through the waves she rises,
  Beyond the breakers' roar
She hears the shouts of the children
  At play on the sandy shore ;

Or sees the ships' sides tower
  Above like a wet black wall ;
Or shouts to the roaring breakers,
  And answers the sea-gull's call.

But down in the quiet waters
  Better she loves to play,
Making a sea-weed garden,
  Purple and green and gray ;

Stringing with pearls a necklace,
  Or learning curious spells
From the water witch, gray and ancient,
  And hearing the tales she tells.

Out in the stable her sea-horse
  Champs in his crystal stall,

And fishes with scales that glisten
   Come leaping forth at her call.

So the little princess
   Is busy and happy all day,
Just as the human children
   Are busy and happy at play.

And when the darkness gathers
   Over the lonely deep,
On a bed of velvet sea-weed
   The princess is rocked to sleep.

Unknown

The Little Land.

When at home alone I sit
And am very tired of it,
I have just to shut my eyes
To go sailing through the skies—
To go sailing far away
To the pleasant Land of Play;
To the fairy land afar
Where the Little People are;

Where the clover-tops are trees,
And the rain-pools are the seas,
And the leaves like little ships
Sail about on tiny trips ;
And above the daisy-tree
    Through the grasses,
High o'erhead the Bumble Bee
    Hums and passes.

In that forest to and fro
I can wander, I can go ;
See the spider and the fly,
And the ants go marching by,
Carrying parcels with their feet
Down the green and grassy street.
I can in the sorrel sit,
Where the ladybird alit.
I can climb the jointed grass ;
    And on high
See the greater swallows pass
    In the sky,
And the round sun rolling by
Heeding no such things as I.

Through that forest I can pass
Till, as in a looking-glass,

Little Things with lovely Eyes

SeeMe sailing with Surprise

Humming fly and daisy-tree
And my tiny self I see,
Painted very clear and neat
On the rain-pool at my feet.
Should a leaflet come to land
Drifting near to where I stand,
Straight I'll board that tiny boat
Round the rain-pool sea to float.
Little thoughtful creatures sit
On the grassy coasts of it ;
Little things with lovely eyes
See me sailing with surprise.
Some are clad in armour green—
(These have sure to battle been !)—
Some are pied with ev'ry hue,
Black and crimson, gold and blue ;
Some have wings and swift are gone ;⸺
But they all look kindly on.

When my eyes I once again
Open, and see all things plain :
High bare walls, great bare floor ;
Great big knobs on drawer and door ;
Great big people, perched on chairs,
Stitching tucks and mending tears,
Each a hill that I could climb,

And talking nonsense all the time—
   O dear me
   That I could be
A sailor on the rain-pool sea,
A climber in the clover-tree,
And just come back, a sleepy-head,
Late at night to go to bed.
               Robert Louis Stevenson

THE WALRUS and THE Carpenter

THE sun was shining on the sea,
    Shining with all his might:
He did his very best to make
    The billows smooth and bright—
And this was odd, because it was
  The middle of the night.

The moon was shining sulkily,
　　Because she thought the sun
Had got no business to be there
　　After the day was done—
" It's very rude of him," she said,
　　" To come and spoil the fun ! "

The sea was wet as wet could be,
　　The sands were dry as dry.
You could not see a cloud, because
　　No cloud was in the sky :
No birds were flying overhead—
　　There were no birds to fly.

The Walrus and the Carpenter
　　Were walking close at hand :
They wept like anything to see
　　Such quantities of sand :
" If this were only cleared away,"
　　They said, " it *would* be grand ! "

" If seven maids with seven mops
　　Swept it for half a year,
Do you suppose," the Walrus said,
　　" That they could get it clear ? "
" I doubt it," said the Carpenter,
　　And shed a bitter tear.

" O Oysters, come and walk with us ! "
  The Walrus did beseech.
" A pleasant walk, a pleasant talk,
  Along the briny beach :
We cannot do with more than four,
  To give a hand to each."

The eldest Oyster looked at him,
  But never a word he said :
The eldest Oyster winked his eye,
  And shook his heavy head—
Meaning to say he did not choose
  To leave the oyster-bed.

But four young Oysters hurried up,
  All eager for the treat :
Their coats were brushed, their faces washed,
  Their shoes were clean and neat—
And this was odd, because, you know,
  They hadn't any feet.

Four other Oysters followed them,
  And yet another four ;
And thick and fast they came at last,
  And more, and more, and more—
All hopping through the frothy waves,
  And scrambling to the shore.

The Walrus and the Carpenter
  Walked on a mile or so,
And then they rested on a rock
  Conveniently low :
And all the little Oysters stood
  And waited in a row.

" The time has come," the Walrus said,
  " To talk of many things :
Of shoes—and ships—and sealing-wax—
  Of cabbages—and kings—
And why the sea is boiling hot—
  And whether pigs have wings."

" But wait a bit," the Oysters cried,
  " Before we have our chat ;
For some of us are out of breath,
  And all of us are fat ! "
" No hurry ! " said the Carpenter.
  They thanked him much for that.

" A loaf of bread," the Walrus said,
  " Is what we chiefly need :
Pepper and vinegar besides
  Are very good indeed—
Now, if you're ready, Oysters dear,
  We can begin to feed."

"But not on us!" the Oysters cried,
 Turning a little blue.
"After such kindness, that would be
 A dismal thing to do!"
"The night is fine," the Walrus said.
 "Do you admire the view?

"It was so kind of you to come!
 And you are very nice!"
The Carpenter said nothing but
 "Cut us another slice.
I wish you were not quite so deaf—
 I've had to ask you twice!"

"It seems a shame," the Walrus said,
 "To play them such a trick.
After we've brought them out so far,
 And made them trot so quick!"
The Carpenter said nothing but
 "The butter's spread too thick!"

"I weep for you," the Walrus said:
 "I deeply sympathize,"
With sobs and tears he sorted out
 Those of the largest size,
Holding his pocket-handkerchief
 Before his streaming eyes.

233

"O Oysters," said the Carpenter,
  "You've had a pleasant run!
Shall we be trotting home again!"
  But answer came there none—
And this was scarcely odd, because
  They'd eaten every one.

Lewis Carroll

The Fairies of the Caldon Low

 N D where have you been, my Mary,
And where have you been from me?"
"I've been to the top of the Caldon
Low,
The midsummer-night to see!"

"And what did you see, my Mary,
  All up on the Caldon Low?"
"I saw the glad sunshine come down,
  And I saw the merry winds blow."

"And what did you hear, my Mary,
  All up on the Caldon Hill?"
"I heard the drops of the waters made,
  And the ears of the green corn fill."

"Oh! tell me all, my Mary,
  All, all that ever you know;
For you must have seen the fairies
  Last night on the Caldon Low."

"Then take me on your knee, mother;
  And listen, mother of mine.
A hundred fairies danced last night,
  And the harpers they were nine.

"And their harp-strings rung so merrily
  To their dancing feet so small;
But oh! the words of their talking
  Were merrier far than all."

" And what were the words, my Mary,
  That then you heard them say?"
" I'll tell you all, my mother;
  But let me have my way.

" Some of them played with the water,
  And rolled it down the hill;
' And this,' they said, ' shall speedily turn
  The poor old miller's mill:

" ' For there has been no water
  Ever since the first of May;
And a busy man will the miller be
  At dawning of the day.

" ' Oh! the miller, how he will laugh
  When he sees the mill-dam rise!
The jolly old miller, how he will laugh,
  Till the tears fill both his eyes!'

" And some they seized the little winds
  That sounded over the hill;
And each put a horn into his mouth,
  And blew both loud and shrill:

" ' And there,' they said, 'the merry winds go,
   Away from every horn ;
And they shall clear the mildew dank
   From the blind old widow's corn.

" ' Oh ! the poor blind widow,
   Though she has been blind so long,
She'll be blithe enough when the mildew's
     gone,
   And the corn stands tall and strong.'

" And some they brought the brown lint-seed,
   And flung it down from the Low;
' And this,' they said, ' by the sunrise,
   In the weaver's croft shall grow.

" ' Oh ! the poor lame weaver,
   How he will laugh outright,
When he sees his dwindling flax-field
   All full of flowers by night ! '

" And then outspoke a brownie,
   With a long beard on his chin ;
' I have spun up all the tow,' said he,
   ' And I want some more to spin.

" 'I've spun a piece of hempen cloth,
  And I want to spin another ;
A little sheet for Mary's bed,
  And an apron for her mother.'

" With that I could not help but laugh,
  And I laughed out loud and free ;
And then on the top of the Caldon Low
  There was no one left but me.

" And all on the top of the Caldon Low
  The mists were cold and grey,
And nothing I saw but the mossy stones
  That round about me lay.

" But coming down from the hill-top,
  I heard afar below.
How busy the jolly miller was
  And how the wheel did go.

" And I peeped into the widow's field,
  And, sure enough, were seen
The yellow ears of the mildewed corn,
  All standing stout and green.

"And down to the weaver's croft I stole,
  To see if the flax were sprung;
But I met the weaver at his gate,
  With the good news on his tongue.

"Now this is all I heard, mother,
  And all that I did see;
So, pr'ythee, make my bed, mother,
  For I'm tired as I can be."

Mary Howitt

A Good Thanksgiving

AID old Gentleman Gay, "On a
  Thanksgiving Day,
  If you want a good time, then give
  something away;"
So he sent a fat turkey to Shoemaker Price,
And the Shoemaker said, "What a big bird!
  how nice!

241

And, since a good dinner's before me, I
    ought
To give poor Widow Lee the small chicken I
    bought."

"This fine chicken, O see!" said the pleased
    Widow Lee,
"And the kindness that sent it, how precious
    to me!
I would like to make some one as happy as I—
I'll give Washwoman Biddy my big pumpkin
    pie."

"And O, sure," Biddy said, "'tis the queen
    of all pies!
Just to look at its yellow face gladdens my
    eyes!
Now it's *my* turn, I think; and a sweet ginger-
    cake
For the motherless Finigan Children I'll
    bake."

"A sweet-cake, all our own! 'Tis too good to
    be true!"
Said the Finigan Children, Rose, Denny, and
    Hugh;

"It smells sweet of spice, and we'll carry a slice
To poor little Lame Jake—who has nothing
    that's nice."

"O, I thank you, and thank you!" said little
    Lame Jake;
"O what bootiful, bootiful, bootiful cake!
And O, such a big slice! I will save all the
    crumbs,
And will give 'em to each little Sparrow that
    comes!"

And the Sparrows they twittered, as if they
    would say,
Like old Gentleman Gay, "On a Thanks-
    giving Day,
If you want a good time, then give something
    away!"

Marian Douglas

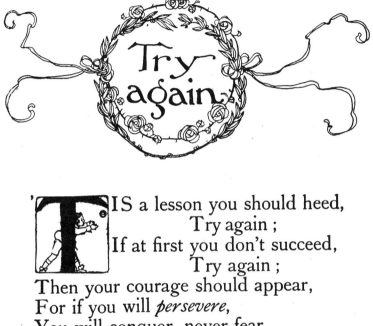

'TIS a lesson you should heed,
  Try again ;
If at first you don't succeed,
  Try again ;
Then your courage should appear,
For if you will *persevere*,
You will conquer, never fear,
  Try again.

Once or twice, though you should fail,
  Try again ;
If you would at last prevail,
  Try again ;

If we strive, 'tis no disgrace
Though we do not win the race;
What should we do in that case?
    Try again.

If you find your task is hard,
    Try again;
Time will bring you your reward,
    Try again;
All that other folk can do,
Why, with patience, may not you?
Only keep this rule in view,
    Try again.   *E. Hickson*

The Grey Squirrels

WHEN in my youth I travellèd
Throughout each north countrie,
Many a strange thing did I hear,
And many a strange thing see.

I sat with small men in their huts,
 Built of the drifted snow;
No fire had we but the seal-oil lamp,
 Nor other light did know.

For far and wide the plains were lost
 For months in the winter dark;
And we heard the growl of the hungry bear,
 And the blue fox's bark.

But when the sun rose redly up
 To shine for half a year,
Round and round through the skies to sail,
 Nor once to disappear,

Then on I went, with curious eyes,
 And saw where, like to man,
The beaver built his palaces;
 And where the ermine ran.

But nothing was there that pleased me more
 Than when, in autumn brown,
I came, in the depths of the pathless woods,
 To the Grey Squirrels' town.